CHEROKEE

OCT 2 - 1990

The Young Scientist Investigates

Rocks and Soil

by
Terry Jennings

CP CHILDRENS PRESS®
CHICAGO

Illustrated by
Norma Burgin
Karen Daws
Gary Hincks
Ed McLachlan
Tony Morris
Tudor Artists

Library of Congress Cataloging-in-Publication Data

Jennings, Terry J.
    Rocks and soil / by Terry Jennings.
      p.   cm. — (The Young scientist investigates.)
    Includes index.
    Summary: An introduction to different kinds of rocks and
soils describing their characteristics, location, and uses. Includes
study questions, activities, and experiments.
    ISBN 0-516-08407-0
    1. Rocks—Juvenile literature. 2. Soils—Juvenile literature.
3. Geology—Experiments—Juvenile literature. [1. Rocks.
2. Soils. 3. Geology—Experiments. 4. Experiments.] I. Title.
II. Series: Jennings, Terry J. Young scientist investigates.
QE432.2.J46   1988
552—dc 19   88-22889
                                   CIP
                                    AC

North American edition published in 1989 by Regensteiner
Publishing Enterprises, Inc.

The Young Scientist Investigates

Rocks and Soil

Contents

The Earth

Many years ago people thought the world was flat. Sailors on long sea journeys were afraid they might fall off the edge. We now know that the Earth is shaped like a round ball. We call this shape a *sphere* or *globe*. We can see the Earth is round when we watch ships gradually come into view over the horizon.

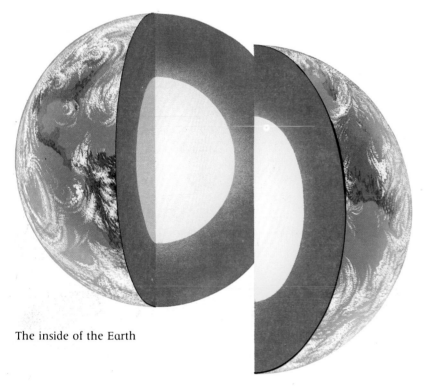

The inside of the Earth

Astronauts have photographed the round Earth many times from out in space. We know the shape of the Earth, but we do not know very much about what it is like inside. We do know the outside of the Earth is covered by a skin of rocks. This skin of rocks is called the Earth's crust. The crust of rocks goes underneath the oceans and seas as well. Deep underneath the crust it is very hot. It is so hot that the rocks are liquid.

Ship coming into sight over the horizon

The Earth as seen from space

Rocks

The Earth we live on is covered with rocks, but in many places the rocks are hidden by soil and plants. We can see the rocks in deserts, mountains and the cliffs by the sea. Rivers wear away the rocks and make deep valleys. Rocks of different colors can be seen in the sides of these valleys. We can also see the rocks when we look at the walls of quarries. Rocks can be seen when mines are dug, or cuttings are made for roads or railways.

Sea cliff

We use rocks for many things. Metals come from rocks, so do coal and oil. Many buildings are made from rocks. Gravestones, memorials and some statues are carved from rock. Small pieces of a very hard rock called granite are used to surface roads. But rocks are not always hard. One of the best known rocks is clay. Clay is used to make bricks and pottery.

Minerals

A rock is made up of chemical substances called minerals. Minerals are made by nature. A few rocks are made up of only one mineral. But most have more than one mineral in them. There are hundreds of kinds of minerals. Some of them make strange and beautiful shapes called *crystals*. A few of them are shown on this page.

Some minerals contain metals. Most metals are found in the ground in mixtures known as ores. One of the common ores of iron is found as golden crystals. It is often called fool's gold . But real gold, as well as silver and platinum, are very rare. Because they are so rare and valuable they are called precious metals.

Some mineral crystals are also hard to find. These are called precious stones. The rarest and most beautiful precious stones are diamonds, emeralds, rubies and sapphires. Precious stones are cut and polished and worn in rings and other jewelry. Minerals, metals and precious stones are things we obtain from rocks.

Some cut and uncut precious stones

Calcite

Fool's Gold

Nugget of real gold

Fluorspar

Quartz crystals with amethyst

Volcanoes

Deep inside the Earth the rock is very hot. Because the rock is so hot it is a liquid. In some parts of the world the Earth's crust is weak and volcanoes are formed. As a volcano erupts, hot liquid rock comes out of the ground. This liquid is called lava. When a volcano has erupted many times, it may build up a cone-shaped mountain. As the hot, liquid lava cools and hardens, beautiful minerals may be made in it. The southeastern Hawaiian islands and the Cascades in Washington and Oregon have active volcanoes.

Granite is a rock which was formed by volcanoes. Granite has beautiful crystals in it which were formed when liquid lava from a volcano cooled. Granite hills and mountains are found in many places in the western United States.

Granite

Some rocks in Northern Ireland are shaped like huge stepping stones. People used to think they were used by giants to get from Ireland to Scotland. They called these rocks the Giant's Causeway. We now know these strange rocks were formed long ago when lava poured from a volcano. Edinburgh Castle is built on an old volcano. So is the castle at Dumbarton, also in Scotland.

The Giant's Causeway

Edinburgh Castle

Glaciers and earthquakes

Rocks show that North America was once much colder than it is now. In some places, such as southeastern Alaska and British Columbia, Canada, there are rivers of ice called glaciers. As the glaciers slide slowly down the mountains, they cut wide valleys shaped like the letter U. When the ice melts it leaves behind little hills of stones and soil that have been pushed by the sliding ice. There are glaciers and many U-shaped valleys in the northwestern Rockies of Montana.

There are many of these U-shaped valleys in the mountain areas of Yosemite Falls, California. There are also many of the little hills of soil and stones that were pushed up by the sliding ice. So we know that California was once much colder and had glaciers. Earthquakes happen very often in California. These earthquakes pushed up some of the rocks of California long ago, as they do today.

Once, the land that is now Wales was at the bottom of the sea. Then a great earthquake pushed the seabed high into the air. Now if you climb a mountain in Wales you may find very old seashells near the top.

Glacier in Switzerland

U-shaped valley

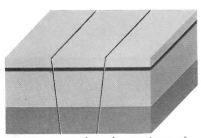
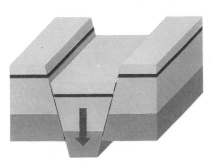
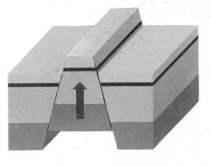
During an earthquake sections of rock may slip or be pushed upwards.

How rocks are broken down

Earthquakes can push up mountains. But many things can wear the mountains down. Eventually even the tallest mountains will be worn away. Wind, ice and rain can wear the mountains away. Plant roots force open cracks in the rocks. Water gets in cracks, freezes, and breaks off pieces of rock. The heat of the sun by day and the cold at night makes rocks break.

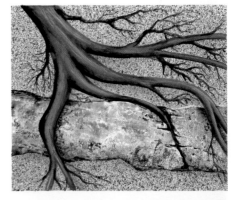

Little pieces of mountain are washed away by streams. The little pieces of rock scratch more rock away. The streams go into rivers, and the rivers flow to the sea, carrying little pieces of rock with them. At the same time, rocks by the sea are being broken down by the waves into pebbles. The pebbles break down into shingle. The shingle breaks down to form sand. The sand grains may break down even more into mud.

Mountain stream carving small valley in rocks

The wearing away of rocky sea cliffs

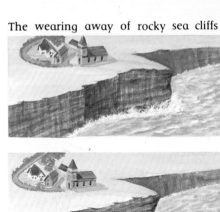

8

How new rocks are formed

Mud, sand and stones pile up at a river mouth

The mud, sand and stones carried by the rivers and waves pile up into thick layers on the bottom of the sea. After thousands of years, they are pressed into new rock. Limestone, chalk, sandstone and clay were all made at the bottom of the sea. They were formed in layers called *strata*. You can see these strata in cliffs and the sides of quarries. Limestone and sandstone are useful rocks for building. They are easy to cut.

Sometimes the rocks formed under the sea are changed by heat, by chemicals, and by other rocks pressing down on them. The rocks formed by volcanoes can also be changed in these ways. All kinds of rocks can be changed. Slate which is sometimes used for roofs was once soft shale. The beautiful rock called marble, which is used for fine buildings, statues and gravestones, was once limestone.

A number of big castles and cathedrals are made from limestone and sandstone. Farmers use ground chalk or limestone to improve the soil. Chalk is also used in cement, concrete, toothpaste and paint.

A sandstone castle

Farmer spreading lime

Slate-roofed houses

9

Fossils

Rocks made at the bottom of the sea often have fossils in them. When an animal or plant dies in soft mud or sand it soon decays. But it sometimes leaves behind a print in the rock, showing how it was shaped. Sometimes the print is filled by more sand and mud, or by minerals. The filling becomes solid and forms a cast. The cast looks just like the original shell, leaf or animal skeleton. It is a fossil.

Fossils can teach us much about animals and plants that lived long ago. We now know that the first horses were no bigger than small dogs. We also know about dinosaurs and other prehistoric animals because of their fossils. Fossil footprints of dinosaurs have been found as well as fossils of their bones.

How a fossil may be formed

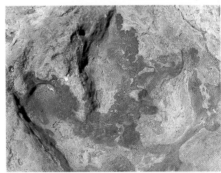

How horses have gradually changed

A fossil dinosaur footprint

Ammonites – fossil snail shells

Fossil leaf

10

Fuels from the Earth

One of the most useful rocks is coal. People burn coal for fuel and they make many chemicals from it. Millions of years ago much of the land was dense forest. The trees and plants died and were covered by mud and sand. Very slowly the mud and sand turned into shale and sandstone. The trees and plants were changed into soft coal. As more and more mud and sand pressed down, the soft coal was changed into hard coal. Seams of coal were found between the layers of sandstone and shale. We can sometimes find fossils of the plants which formed coal. Huge machines are used to dig up the coal near the surface. The seams deeper down are dug by miners working in tunnels.

Oil is another fuel found in the Earth's rocks. It was made from tiny sea creatures that lived millions of years ago. When these creatures died they sank to the seabed. They were buried by mud and sand. Over millions of years they turned into tiny drops of oil. In some places the rocks have bent and the oil has been trapped in large underground lakes. When men drill through the rocks, they find the oil. There is often gas with the oil which can also be used as a fuel.

How coal is formed

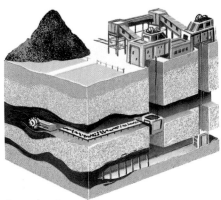

A coal mine

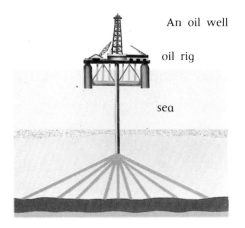

An oil well

oil rig

sea

Small living things like these formed oil.

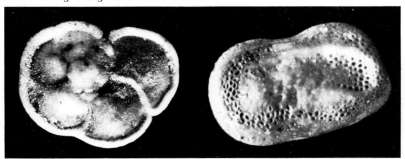

11

Do you remember?

(Look for the answers in the part of the book you have just been reading if you do not know them.)

1 What do we call the shape of the Earth?

2 What is the name given to the skin of rocks that cover the outside of the Earth?

3 Make a list of some of the things for which we use rocks.

4 Name a rock that is very soft.

5 What are the substances called that make up a rock?

6 Why are gold, silver, and platinum called precious metals?

7 Name some precious stones.

8 What is it like deep inside the Earth?

9 Where are volcanoes found?

10 What is the hot liquid called that comes out of a volcano?

11 Where was granite formed?

12 What are glaciers like and where are they found?

13 What shape are the valleys made by glaciers?

14 What do earthquakes sometimes do to rocks?

15 Make a list of some of the things that can wear rocks away.

16 What happens to the mud, sand, and stones carried by the rivers and waves, and what may they form?

17 Name two rocks that were formed at the bottom of the sea.

18 How can rocks be changed?

19 What can we learn from studying fossils?

20 What were coal and oil formed from?

Things to do

1 **Make a collection of rocks.** Look for pebbles and pieces of rock in the garden, at the seaside, by the roadside and in the country. River banks, the beds of streams, road cuttings, old quarries and building sites can also produce rock samples. **These last places are dangerous, though.** *Do not go to them without permission, and always go with a grown-up.*

Wash your rocks and pebbles carefully and dry them. Label each one with the name of the place where you found it and the date.

12

Look at each pebble or piece of rock carefully, using a hand lens or magnifying glass. What color is each one? Is it rough or smooth to the touch? Does it appear to be made of grains? Is the specimen made of crystals?

Is the rock or pebble made up of all the same materials? Will the rock soak up water? Are there any fossils in it?

How hard or soft is each rock or pebble? One of the best ways to test for hardness is to try to scratch your rock with different things. Try your fingernail first. If you cannot scratch the rock with your fingernail, try to scratch it with a coin. Next, try to scratch the rock or pebble with a penknife blade or the blade of a screwdriver. If the rock still will not scratch, try a steel file.

If you have one, it is a good idea to fix your rock in the vice on a workbench. Then you will not scratch or cut yourself when you see how hard or soft your rocks are.

When you are searching for rock specimens, always keep a lookout for fossils. Make a collection of these as well. Carefully clean and wash each one. Label it saying where and when you found it.

Use books to try to find the names of your rocks and fossils.

2   Visit your local museum. Ask to see their collection of rocks, minerals and fossils. How many of the rocks, minerals and fossils were found locally, and how many were found a long way away? You may be able to find out the names of some of the rocks and fossils in your own collection if you compare them with those at the museum.

3   Make a collection. Find pictures of different kinds of jewelry, precious stones, and things made of precious metals.

Choose one of the pieces of jewelry you like the best. Write a poem about it.

Make some music to go with the poem. Will it be a happy tune or a sad tune? Write your music down if you can.

4   Collect pictures of all the wonderful scenery in the world in which rocks can be seen. Include hills, mountains, river valleys, waterfalls, cliffs, beaches, caves, deserts, volcanoes and glaciers.

5   Make a book. Describe all the things we use rocks for. Collect as many interesting pictures as you can to illustrate your book. Draw some pictures of your own.

6   Whereabouts in the world are volcanoes found? Mark the places on a map of the world. Do the marks make a pattern? Whereabouts in the world do earthquakes happen? Mark these on the map as well. Do the marks showing where earthquakes happen make a pattern? Do earthquakes happen in the same parts of the world as volcanoes?

7   Make crystals like those formed by some minerals. Add salt to some warm water in a clean jam jar. Stir the salt until it dissolves. Keep adding salt to the water

until no more salt will dissolve. You have now made a strong salt solution.

Pour a little of the salt solution into a clean saucer and leave it on a windowsill. When all the water has evaporated, look with a hand lens or magnifying glass at what is left in the saucer. What do you notice?

If you want to make big crystals, evaporate your salt solution very slowly.

Make some more crystals in the same way. Try sugar, washing detergent, alum, lemonade powder, and Epsom salts. Alum and Epsom salts can be bought quite cheaply from a pharmacy.

8 Find out about fuels. Ask the other children in your class how many of their houses are heated by solid fuel (coal, coke, etc.), gas, electricity, or oil.

Make a bar chart of your findings. Which fuel is the most popular? Ask the people in your class which fuel they like the best. Why? Write down the reasons they give.

9 Make a model volcano. Make the cone of the volcano with clay or plaster of

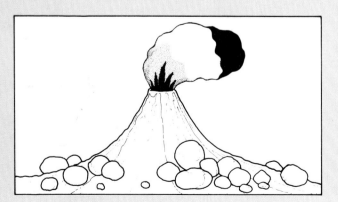

Paris. Do not forget to make a hole in the top of the volcano for the crater.

Take a tuft of cotton wool. Paint it red, orange and black. Stick it in the crater of the volcano. The cotton wool can be the smoke and flames coming from the volcano.

10 Collect pictures of the damage done by earthquakes and volcanoes. Make a wall chart with your pictures.

11 Find out the names of as many metals as you can. Write their names across a sheet of paper and then draw columns underneath them.

Find out as many things as possible that are made of these different metals. Write their names in the columns under the names of the metals.

Which countries do the different metals come from? How are the metals obtained from the ground?

What substances are sometimes used instead of the metals nowadays? Why?

12 Make model fossils using plaster of Paris. Or if a friend will lend you a real fossil from his or her collection, you can make a copy of it.

Roll out some clay until it makes a flat sheet about $1/3$ to $3/4$ of an inch thick.

Take the specimen you want to make the plaster cast of, and gently press it into the clay, using a flat piece of wood or an old rolling pin. As well as fossils you could

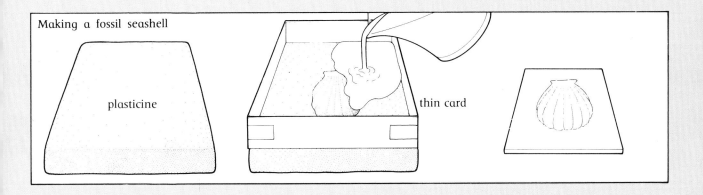

Making a fossil seashell

plasticine   thin card

make casts of tree leaves and twigs, and seashells such as cockles and top shells which have interesting shapes. Even finger prints would make interesting casts.

Carefully remove your specimen from the clay. See that you have a clear impression of it in the clay, if not start again. Make a wall around the impression of the specimen using a strip of index card about ¾ of an inch wide. Fasten the ends of the card with tape or a paper clip.

Put some water into an old jam jar or an old jug. Add a spoonful of plaster of Paris powder to the water and stir it with a clean stick. Keep adding powder and stirring until the mixture feels like thin custard.

Carefully pour the liquid plaster into the wall of cardboard, tapping out any air bubbles as they form. Level the plaster off with the top of the card. Leave the plaster for at least 30 minutes to set. Then carefully peel off the card.

The next day peel off the clay. Gently brush your plaster cast with a soft brush until it is clean. Paint your plaster cast with poster paint and label it.

If you wish to hang up your plaster cast, you should put a loop of wire or string in the plaster cast while it is still wet.

13 Collect pictures of prehistoric animals and make a wall chart with them. Which is your favorite prehistoric animal? Why? Write a story about your favorite prehistoric animal. Make some music to go with your story. Write the music down if you can.

14 Use your imagination. One day you are out for a walk in a lonely part of the country when suddenly you feel the ground beneath your feet rumbling and shaking. From a crack in a nearby rock you see smoke and sparks drifting upwards. Have you discovered a new volcano?

Write a story about your adventures. Describe what the countryside is like, what you see, how you feel, and what you do.

Can you think of a funny or unusual explanation for the ground rumbling and shaking, and for the smoke and sparks coming from the rocks? Include this in your story.

Soil

Almost everywhere on land there is soil. Sometimes there is a lot of soil. In rocky places there is often very little soil. Some soils are poor and few plants will grow in them. Other soils are good and grow many plants. We say a good soil which grows many plants is *fertile*.

Soil is very valuable to us. All the plants we eat grow in soil. So do the cotton and flax plants that provide us with the materials for some of our clothing. The trees that give us timber and paper grow in the soil. Our meat and milk comes from animals that feed on plants that grow in the soil. Wool and leather also come from these animals. Without soil we would have nothing to eat or read, nothing to write on, and little to wear. Nor would we have any of the things which are made from timber.

Clearing a forest for timber

A field of cotton plants

How soil is formed

All our soil was made from rocks. Frost and plant roots crack the rocks. Streams and rivers wash pieces away. The sea batters rocks and breaks them up. Small pieces of sand blown by the wind scratch soft rocks and break pieces off. All these small pieces of rock may stay where they are. Or they may be carried by the wind, rivers, streams and the waves to other places. In some countries glaciers break off pieces of rock and push them along.

The tiny pieces of rock are not soil, though. But small plants can grow in the pieces of rock. Mosses and lichens can often be seen growing on pieces of rock. When these simple plants die, bacteria and molds grow on them. The dead plants decay and break up into little pieces. The decayed pieces of plant make food for other plants and also for animals. Soon the rock has a lot of black pieces of decayed plants and animals in it. The black substance is called humus. When there is a lot of humus mixed in with tiny pieces or grains of rock, a soil has been formed.

Mosses and lichens growing on a rock

How soil is formed

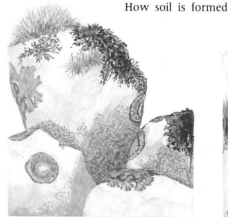

Different kinds of soil

There are many different kinds of soils. Some soils are formed where the ground is always wet. These are not very fertile. Because the ground is so wet, there is not enough air for plant roots to breathe and grow properly. The soils formed under pine trees and heather are not very fertile either. In deserts plants do not grow long enough for soil to form. Plants appear only after the rare and sudden rainstorms.

Soil washed away from a hillside where too many animals have been put out to graze

Heather

Desert

Oak wood

The most fertile soils are found under grassland and under the forests of broad-leaved trees such as oak and maple. These soils can also grow very good crops if they are cleared of the grass or trees and are tended carefully. But people have often been careless about the soil. They have removed the trees and plants that hold the soil in place on hills. The soil is then easily washed or blown away. People have put too many animals out to graze, and the animals have eaten all the plants. Hedges have been cut down so that the soil blows away in dry weather. Many of the world's deserts were once fertile. They have been turned into deserts because people were careless.

Deep fertile soil underneath a tree

Plants growing in very wet ground

Sandy soils and clay soils

Some soils are made of grains of rock that are just big enough to see. You can feel the little grains when you rub the soil between your fingers. This is a sandy soil. A sandy soil is easy to dig. When it rains the water runs through a sandy soil quickly. Sometimes in dry weather the plants growing on a sandy soil do not have enough water. Then they may die.

Sandy soil (above) and clay soil (below) as seen through a magnifying glass

Some soils are made from pieces of rock so small that you cannot see them. If you rub the soil between your fingers it feels sticky like soap. You can press it between your fingers into a ball. A soil that is made from these minute pieces of rock is called a clay soil. Digging a clay soil is very hard work. It is even harder to dig a clay soil when it is wet. Water does not pass through a clay soil very easily. So a shovelful of clay soil is very heavy. When the weather is dry, big cracks may form in a clay soil. Plant roots near these cracks often dry out and die.

Clay soil cracking when dry

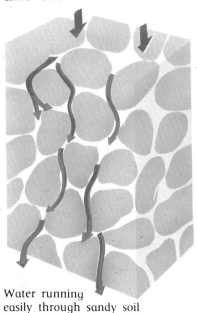

Water running easily through sandy soil

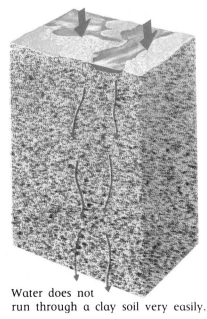

Water does not run through a clay soil very easily.

20

Loam

Humus

Clay Sand

The best kind of soil is called a loam. It has as much clay as sand in it. It also has a lot of humus in it. A loam is quite easy to dig. It does not dry out very quickly in hot weather. It has a lot of food for the plants. Plants grow well in a loam soil. Loam is also a home for many kinds of plants and animals. So are other kinds of soils.

Some quite large animals such as rabbits, badgers, moles and mice have their homes in the soil. But many of the plants and animals living in the soil are very tiny. The common tiny plants in the soil are bacteria. These are so small that they can be seen only with a powerful microscope. There may be millions of bacteria in a handful of soil. When plants and animals die, the bacteria help to make the plants and animals decay in the soil to form humus. Further decay makes the humus break down into the mineral salts from which the dead plants and animals were made. These mineral salts go into the ground and make food for new plants.

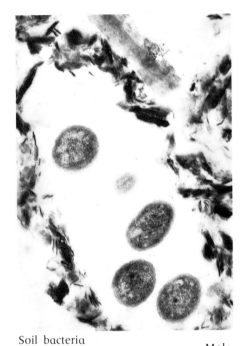

Soil bacteria

Mole

Rabbit

Earthworms

One of the most important animals in the soil is the earthworm. A fertile soil may contain many earthworms. But you do not often see them as they do not like the light and stay in their burrows during the day. At night, however, they come to the surface. Worms eat soil to get from it the small pieces of decaying plant and animal food they need. The soil passes through their bodies and comes out as worm casts. Sometimes you can see these worm casts on the surface, but often they are produced underground.

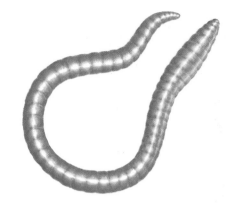

Earthworm

Earthworms also pull dead leaves into the soil. There the leaves decay and form humus. Earthworms are good for the soil because they mix it up and break it into fine pieces. Their burrows let air into the soil, so that plant roots can breathe and grow better. The worm burrows also allow water to drain away. Plants grow well in soils which have plenty of earthworms in them.

Worm cast

Plant foods

As plants grow they take water from the soil. They also take mineral salts from the soil. When the plants die, the mineral salts go back into the soil. So the same mineral salts are used over and over again. But if the plants are taken away to be eaten by people, then the mineral salts do not go back into the soil. When a farmer takes plants from a field, he is taking away mineral salts.

Good farmers and gardeners put mineral salts back into the soil. They put manures or fertilizers onto the soil. Manure is the waste matter produced by animals. Manure has a lot of mineral salts in it. It also decays to form humus. But there is not enough manure for all the fields. Many farmers and gardeners use chemicals called fertilizers. Fertilizers are clean and they do not smell. They contain a lot of mineral salts. Farmers use special machines to put fertilizers and manures on their fields.

Manure being spread on a field

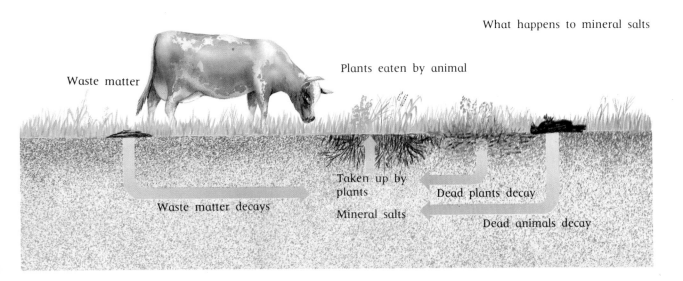

What happens to mineral salts

Waste matter

Plants eaten by animal

Waste matter decays

Taken up by plants

Mineral salts

Dead plants decay

Dead animals decay

23

Taking care of the soil

Farmers plow the fields before they plant them. The plow turns the soil over. This lets air into the soil so that the bacteria, earthworms, and plant roots can breathe. The air allows the plant roots to grow better. Weeds are buried when the soil is plowed. The weeds decay and form humus.

In winter the water in the soil turns to ice. As the water turns to ice it breaks the big lumps of soil into small pieces. When the farmer plants his seeds they grow better in the small pieces of soil. Gardeners use a spade to break the soil, to let air into it and to bury the weeds.

Farm in winter

Plowing

Building on farmland

Soil is very precious because we depend upon it for our food and many other things. Yet every year much of the good soil is covered with buildings, concrete, and roads. We shall have to begin to take much more care of the soil that is left. Fertile soils have taken thousands of years to form.

A new town is built on farmland.

Do you remember?

1 What do we call a soil in which many plants grow?

2 Make a list of some of the things we obtain from the soil.

3 What is all our soil made from?

4 What do we call the black pieces of decayed plants and animals in the soil?

5 Why is soil not formed in the desert?

6 Under what kinds of plants can fertile soil be found?

7 In what ways have people been careless with the soil, allowing it to be washed or blown away?

8 What is a sandy soil like?

9 How could you recognize a clay soil?

10 Which is the hardest soil to dig: a clay soil or a sandy soil?

11 What is the best kind of soil called? What does it contain?

12 Name some large animals that have their homes in the soil.

13 How do bacteria help to improve the soil?

14 How do earthworms help to improve the soil?

15 What do plants take from the soil as they grow, besides mineral salts?

16 How can mineral salts be lost from the soil?

17 How do farmers and gardeners put mineral salts back into their soil?

18 What does manure decay to form?

19 How does plowing make the soil better?

20 What happens to big lumps of soil when the cold winter weather comes?

Things to do

1 **Find out about the content of soil.** Put a handful of garden soil in a jar with straight sides. A clear glass coffee jar is a good one to use. Then pour in water until the jar is about three-quarters full.

Put the lid on the jar and shake it really well. As soon as you have stopped shaking it, put the jar on a table or windowsill and watch carefully to see how the soil settles.

How long does it take for the water to clear? Can you see the layers of the different sized pieces? How many layers can you see?

Which layer has the largest pieces?

Which layer has the smallest pieces? Measure the thickness of each of the layers.

Are there any little pieces of humus and decaying plants and animals floating on the top of the water? These usually look black.

Do the same thing with soils from other places. If you always use the same kind of jar you can make a table to compare the thicknesses and colors of the different layers in the different soils.

You could also make drawings of the jars containing each of the different soils.

2   Finding animals in soil. Collect a small plastic bagful of the soil which is beneath the layer of dead leaves in a wood or under a hedge or tree. Spread some newspapers over the table.

Pour the soil out onto the paper. Carefully look at the soil with a hand lens or magnifying glass.

Collect small animals that you find and put them in a jam jar. How many animals of each kind are there? Draw one of each. Watch to see how many legs and wings each animal has. How does it move?

When you have finished with these small animals, put them back in the wood or under the hedge or tree they came from.

3   Make a soil profile. Find a tin lid. Roll a sheet of plastic wrap into a tube which fits neatly into the tin lid. Seal the plastic into a roll with tape.

Ask permission to dig a hole in the garden. Dig a hole that is as deep as your tube is long. Dig the hole carefully and clean the sides of all loose soil.

Put a little of the soil from the bottom of your hole in the bottom of the tube. Then take some of the soil that is a few inches from the bottom of your hole and put that in the tube. Do this until your tube shows exactly how the soil in the sides of your hole changes.

Look at the soil profile in the tube carefully. Where is the darkest soil to be found? Where is the lightest soil? Where are the most stones? How far down do plant roots grow?

Compare your soil profile with those from your friends' gardens. Are they all the same?

4   Find out why we dig gardens. Dig a hole in the garden with a shovel. Carefully put all the soil you take out of the hole onto sheets of plastic or thick paper.

Now carefully put the soil back into the hole without treading on any of it. Can you get all the soil back into the hole?

If you cannot get all the soil back into the hole, what has made the soil take up more room? Why is this important? Would the same thing happen if a garden was being dug normally or if a field was being plowed?

5   Find out all you can about earthworms. Carefully take an earthworm and put it on a sheet of paper. How many inches long is the worm when it stretches itself out? How long is it when it draws itself up?

What shape is the worm? What color is it?

Gently turn the worm over. Is it the same color underneath?

How many rings are there along the body of the worm?

Do all worms have the same number of rings?

How does the earthworm's head differ from its tail?

Look at the head end of the worm with a magnifying glass or hand lens. Has it got a mouth, nose, ears, or eyes?

What is the thin red line all the way down the worm's back? What does the skin of your worm feel like?

How does the worm move? Put your ear close to the piece of paper on which you have placed the worm. What can you hear? Use a magnifying glass or hand lens to try to find out what is making the noise. Make drawings to show how the shape of the earthworm changes as it moves along.

Make a book about earthworms.

6   Make a wormery . Find a large clear glass jar. Put in some layers of different soils. Make sure that the soils are fine and not too hard or lumpy. Remove any stones. You might also put in a thin layer of sand, chalk or peat.

Keep the soils in the jar moist but not very wet. Put in three or four earthworms. Lay two or three leaves on the surface of

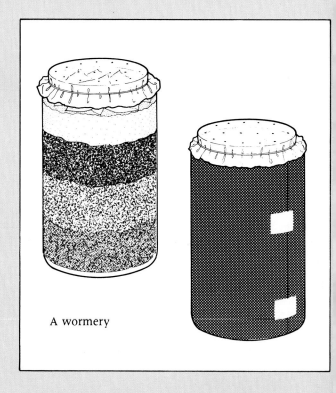

A wormery

the soil in the jar. Cover the jar with a thin piece of plastic wrap in which you have made a few small pinholes to let air through for the worms to breathe.

Cover the outside of the jar with a piece of black paper or thin dark index card. Keep the wormery in a cool dark place.

After a week, slide up the cover to see what the worms have done to the layers of soil. What has happened to the leaves you left on top of the jar? What are the earthworms' burrows like? Are there any worm casts to be seen?

7   Visit a building site. Ask a grown-up to take you to a building site. Look at the tools used for digging holes. Make lists of the tools used for loosening the soil and of the machines which are used to carry away the soil and rock.

Experiments to try

Make some models or pictures of the machines you see.

Why do people dig holes in the roads and on building sites?

8 Make a collection of soils. The color of soil varies from place to place.

Whenever you go on vacation or on visits to friends and relatives, collect a few ounces of the soil. Allow the soil to dry and sieve it or pick out any stones or lumps.

Put the soil either in a small clear, glass or plastic bottle of the kind aspirin is sold in. Label the bottle with where and when you collected the soil. Or put your soil in thin layers in a tall, thin clear glass bottle. Many wine bottles are ideal. Label each layer with where and when you collected it.

Make a collection of sands in a similar way.

9 Use your imagination. In the United States, the most common earthworm is 10 inches long. In some tropical areas of Australia, worms of up to 11 feet in length are found. Their bodies are as thick as a grown-up's finger.

Pretend you are on a visit to Australia when you come across one of these giant earthworms. Describe how you feel and what you do? Are you frightened? Write a story about the giant earthworm and the part of Australia in which you found it.

Do your experiments carefully. Write or draw what you have done and what happens. Say what you have learned. Compare your findings with those of your friends.

1 Rocks and frost

What you need: A small plastic bottle with a screw top (e.g. an empty aspirin bottle); a piece of sandstone, chalk or limestone; a small piece of concrete; a piece of brick; access to a freezer.

What you do: Fill the bottle completely full with water and screw the cap on tightly. Put the bottle in the freezer overnight. What has happened to the bottle the next day? Why?

Put a small piece of sandstone, chalk, or limestone in a bowl of water overnight. Then place the piece of rock on a tin lid and stand it in the freezer overnight. See what has happened the next day.

Try this experiment with other kinds of rocks and building materials, including small pieces of concrete and brick.

Can you think why, after a really hard winter, the roads and pavements sometimes have large potholes and cracks in them?

2 Water and soils

What you need: Two funnels; some filter paper or some cotton wool; some bricks or blocks of wood; a measuring cup; some clean jam jars; at least two different kinds of soils (if possible include a sandy soil and a clay soil); a watch or clock with a second hand.

What you do: Keep your soil samples separate. Spread them out on trays or newspapers and leave them to dry for two or three days. Break up any lumps and pick out any stones. When the soils are dry, crush them with a flat piece of wood until they are like powder.

Set up the two funnels between bricks or blocks of wood. Either put a small tuft of cotton wool in each funnel or line them with filter paper or blotting paper.

Put the same amount of each of two different soils in the two funnels. If possible put a sandy soil in one funnel and a clayey soil in the other.

Put a clean jam jar under each of the two funnels.

Half fill another two jam jars with water. See that each jar contains exactly the same amount of water.

Ask a friend to help you. At a given signal pour water from the two jars into the two funnels. Pour the water slowly so that it does not splash or overflow.

How long does the water take to flow through the two lots of soil? How much water comes out into the jars at the bottom? Is it the same amount of water that you put in? If not where has the water gone?

Which soil lets water through the quickest? Which soil lets the most water through in the end? Which soil would you rather grow plants in in your garden? Why?

Now compare other kinds of soils.

3   Experiments with earthworms

What you need: A wormery (like that on page 28); a variety of plant foods such as raw carrot, potato, onion, apple peel, celery, bread, cookies, fresh vegetable, tree leaves, decaying leaves, etc; a flashlight; piece of index card; a pair of scissors; some newspaper.

What you do: Find out what foods worms like to eat the best. Put small bits of some of the foods on top of the soil in the wormery. Keep the soil in the wormery moist.

Leave the wormery in a cool and dark place for a week. At the end of the week look and see what has happened. Which foods do the worms seem to like the best? Which foods do they like the least?

Now try another selection of foods.

How do earthworms react to light? For this experiment you will need to work in a darkened room or cupboard. Make a small slit in a piece of index card and tape the card to the glass of a flashlight. When the flashlight is switched on you should have a narrow beam of light.

Place a worm on a sheet of wet newspaper in the dark. Let the worm settle down for a while. Then shine the light on the worm's head end. What happens? Now shine the light on the worm's tail end and see what happens. Now try the sides and the middle of the worm in turn. How does the worm react? What does it do?

Place an earthworm on a sheet of paper in a room in which there is a radio, a television, a record player or a piano. When the worm has settled down, play some loud music. Watch the worm carefully. What does it do?

Stop the music and then place the worm on a sheet of paper on top of the radio, television set, record player or piano. When the worm has settled down play some loud music. What does the worm do?

Does the worm behave differently when it is actually on the thing making the music rather than being near it? Can you explain why?

4 How does the kind of soil affect the way in which plants grow?

What you need: A trowel or a shovel; a small quantity of soil from several different places – from under grass, from under trees, from different gardens; some small plant pots or some clean yogurt cup; some mustard seeds.

What you do: Dig a hole in the garden about 12 to 15 inches deep. Fill one plant pot or yogurt cup with soil from the bottom of the hole, and another one from the surface of the ground.

Look at the two soil samples with a hand lens or magnifying glass. What color are they? What do they feel like? What do they smell like? Are there any other differences between the two samples of soil?

Sprinkle mustard seeds on the soil in both pots. Gently press the seeds into the soil with your fingers or with a small piece of flat wood.

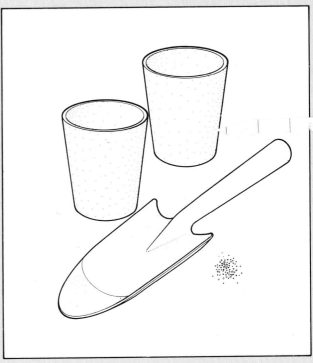

Keep both pots watered regularly, using the same amount of water for each pot.

In which pot do the seeds grow best? Can you think why this might be?

If farmers and gardeners plow or dig very deeply will they grow better crops?

Fill some more pots with the soils from different places. Sprinkle a few mustard seeds onto the surface of the soil. Gently press the seeds into the soil.

Keep all the pots watered regularly, using the same amount of water for each pot.

In which kind of soil does the mustard grow best? Draw a picture to show what the little mustard plants in each pot look like.

Try this experiment with other kinds of seeds: lettuce and radish seeds would be good ones to start with.

Glossary

Here are the meanings of some words which you might have met for the first time in this book.

Bacteria: tiny plants too small to be seen without a powerful microscope. Many bacteria cause materials to decay, a few cause diseases.

Crust: the skin of rocks on the outside of the Earth.

Crystal: the strange and beautiful shapes in which minerals and some chemical substances are found.

Earthquake: a movement of the Earth's crust that can sometimes cause great damage.

Fertile: a good soil that grows many plants is said to be fertile.

Fertilizer: a chemical substance put on the soil to make plants grow better.

Fossil: the preserved imprint of a plant or animal found in rock, or the preserved hard parts of the plant or animal itself.

Glaciers: rivers of ice that occur in some cold countries.

Globe: a shape like that of the Earth or a ball.

Humus: the decayed plant and animal remains found in the soil.

Lava: the hot, liquid rock that comes out of a volcano.

Loam: a fertile soil formed from roughly equal amounts of sand and clay mixed with humus.

Manure: the waste matter produced by animals that is put on the soil to make plants grow better. Manure contains mineral salts and it decays to form humus.

Minerals: the chemical substances that make up rocks.

Mineral salts: the chemical substances that plants obtain from the soil and use as food.

Rock: the solid part of the Earth's crust underneath the soil. Not all rocks are hard: clay is a rock.

Soil: the layer of grains of rock mixed with humus in which plants grow.

Sphere: a shape like that of a ball or the Earth.

Stratum: one of the layers of rocks formed under the sea. If there is more than one layer the word strata is used.

Volcano: a weak part of the Earth's crust through which molten rock or lava from inside the Earth comes out.

Acknowledgments

The publishers would like to thank the following for permission to reproduce transparencies:

Heather Angel p. 16 (left), p. 19 (top); Camera Press p. 3; Bruce Coleman: Jane Burton p. 10 (left), p. 16 (bottom right); Colorific: Penny Tweedie p. 9 (bottom left); Institute of Geological Sciences p. 5, p. 6 (top and bottom right), p. 10 (bottom right); T. Jennings p. 4 (top right and bottom right), p. 7 (bottom), p. 8, p. 9 (right), p. 17, p. 18, p. 19 (bottom); Eric Kay p. 6 (left); Oxford Scientific Films p. 20 (bottom); Picturepoint p. 24 (bottom right); M G Poulton p. 24 (left); Rothamsted Experimental Station p. 20; Shell p. 11; A Smith p. 9 (top); A Souster p. 25; Swiss National Tourist Office p. 7 (top); G C Telling p. 4 (center right); University of Bristol p. 21; ZEFA p. 4 (left), p. 10 (top right), p. 16 (top right), p. 23, p. 24 (top right).

Illustrated by
Norma Burgin, Karen Daws, Gary Hincks, Ed McLachlan, Tony Morris, and Tudor Artists.

Index